simplify
structure
succeed

The practical toolkit for modern life

© 2012, Shannah Kennedy
2nd Edition
Published by The Messenger Group Pty Ltd

PO Box H241
Australia Square NSW 1215

A CIP catalogue of this book is available from the National Library of Australia.

Kennedy, Shannah

Simplify Structure Succeed
ISBN 978-0-9805112-9-1

Published and Project Managed by The Messenger Group

The Messenger Group
Project Manager: Jade Dunwoody
Editorial: Sarah Megginson
Creative: Claire Cassey

www.themessengergroup.com.au

Printed in China

This book is dedicated to my husband Michael who inspires, supports and challenges me to step out of my comfort zone and gives me the freedom and motivation to follow my dreams.

Also, to my beautiful children, Jack and Mia, who remind me what life is about with each golden moment we share. Daily I am grateful, inspired and committed to our great bond.

The answers are all within us when we ask the right questions. So, this book is also dedicated to every person who has the courage to come back to their foundations and take control of their lives. It is dedicated to keeping you connected with who you are, so you can make the best choices and enjoy every success in life.

"When you're so busy being busy, it's easy to lose track of who you are and what is most important to you. Temptations, distractions and obligations are everywhere, so finding the path towards a genuine life requires more than luck. You need to stop. Pick up a pen and paper, open this book, and invest in the positive direction of your life. The process is liberating!"

— Alisa Camplin, OAM, Olympic Gold Medallist

START 14

The first step in this journey begins with self-recognition by discovering who you are at your core. This section will discuss how to cherish each moment, acknowledge and learn from your mistakes and celebrate your major achievements for optimal growth. This is achieved through a rich voyage to identify your values in order to guide and shape your decisions, as well as your habits.

SIMPLIFY 48

Simplicity is one of the most valuable qualities you can strive to embrace. To achieve your goals, you need to rid the clutter from your daily life and with these simple strategies, you can simplify your routines, free your mind and create clear objectives. From there you can achieve balance and start to build a structure to support your vision for the future.

STRUCTURE   88

Having the right structure in place gives you balance and clarity to work towards accomplishing your goals. For this to occur, every part of your life needs to be supported with the help of a planner to manage your time, tasks and obligations efficiently. When identifying how to plan your goals you will also learn to use all of your five senses, take responsibility for your circumstances and recognise your commitment level to move forward.

SUCCEED   126

Your success is your vision and your definition. To achieve your recipe for success, it's important to create a success toolkit, which includes a 20-year plan with a vision of your desired life. Finally, you must harness your strategy for success and celebrate each step in your exciting progression towards optimal living.

A NOTE FROM SHANNAH

Throughout my years of coaching, I've found that my clients share one commonality — most of them don't need motivation. They're very successful people and they know what they need to do to reach their goals.

What they actually need is for things to be simplified, so they can dig themselves out of the clutter to find clarity and purpose in their daily routines, and live a full life without self-destruction.

They want to get back to the foundations of who they are. Here is where all the answers are found.

I have mastered the art of finding this clarity and balance in my life, while also challenging my own comfort zones, committing to relationships, communicating for results and having fun along the way. It is something I commit to on a daily basis, which keeps me motivated and focused and loving what life has to offer.

My business is all about offering new perspective to my clients and companies so they can enjoy the same. And with this book, I am sharing some of my time-proven techniques with you in the hope they will inspire you to turn your goals and dreams for your life, career and business into reality.

My life has been a truly big journey! When I saw the movie *Wall Street* in 1987, I was 17 and trying to decide what to do with my life. All of that power, wealth and success was hugely appealing to my adolescent self, so I committed to getting a job at a high-profile stockbroking firm and succeeded. After a few years there, I decided to gain more life experience.

At age 21, I left to explore the world for two years. I backpacked through Europe, the Middle East and parts of Africa, working my way through kitchens and bars. This was an incredible time in my life. I slept under the stars high in the Atlas Mountains of Morocco, dozed on a small wooden boat on the river Nile, swam in the Dead Sea, and waitressed in

the ski resort of Mürren, Switzerland, home of the James Bond 007 revolving restaurant. I hitchhiked through Spain and slept on many rooftops and stayed in the most basic rooms to the odd amazing hotel or castle.

I then returned to the same stockbroking firm, but I didn't feel challenged. Being true to myself, I decided to leave the industry of figures, numbers and stress, and started working as a PA in a golf management company. Here I really learnt about running a business from the ground up and becoming a true time manager. Negotiating contracts, managing professional golfers, travelling on tour, organising corporate golf days — it was a time of major growth in my life.

Then, a game changer. I was approached by a high profile sports eyewear company to be their sponsorship and PR manager. Instead of managing a dozen golfers, I was working with more than 100 world-class athletes in Australia and internationally. By most people's definition of success, I was living the dream. It was exhilarating, satisfying and demanding all at once. It was also intense.

For most high achievers, life is overloaded and that was definitely the case for me. For several years, I brushed aside the creeping symptoms of burnout — fatigue, stress, exhaustion — and chalked it up as "the price to be paid" for having a successful career. Then, I was delivered a devastating reminder that I needed to slow down. It was July 1999 and I'd just returned from another week-long trip when my body abruptly gave way to chronic fatigue.

It was severely debilitating. I was virtually bed-ridden for 12 months, and as a result, I lost myself, my networks, and my ability to do anything I put my mind to, as my body would not respond. Not surprisingly, I started to experience the beginnings of depression. I felt like such a failure. It was only years later that I realised what a blessing my illness was — a gift that allowed me to see life's grand picture. Recovery was slow, but working with a life coach, I eventually gained the energy, clarity and motivation to bounce back. Rebuilding my life, brick by brick, it took three years to recover completely. Through my career, I had also watched athletes self-destruct once their sporting careers were over. This inspired me to study coaching and teach them how to be whole people, with a purpose and vision for creating life after their short athletic careers ended.

I became an Advanced Certified Coach, and a decade on, it's my desire to manage time so that it works for us rather than against us that places my services in constant demand with high achievers. I have also prioritised and continue to commit to my own self-development, hiring coaches worldwide to train me personally.

Working within large corporations coaching senior executives, sales teams, and also individual business owners, employees and contractors, I always focus on the foundations. It is here the answers lie, because it is by going back to the basics, the fundamentals, that you can gain back some control and make clear, informed decisions.

Over the years, the structures outlined in this book have given insight and added to employee engagement strategies, inspired valuable team building activities and provided powerful tools to connect leaders with their teams.

While these tools are effective in lifting the spirits and energy levels in staff, they are just as effective for managers, leaders, entrepreneurs, athletes, small business owners, and in fact just about anyone who wants to set and achieve clear goals, re-engage with their career path, foster meaningful relationships and live each day to the fullest.

This book is for your life strategy, to help you get back to your foundations, to understand how to be your best and prepare your future so it is clear, inspiring and gives you a great sense of achievement.

Yours in optimal living,

Shannah

P.S. Remember, it is not just about what you get by accomplishing your goals and achieving success, but also about who you become through the process...

"There is only one success –
to be able to spend your life in your
own way."

- Christopher Morley

THE SECRET TO SUCCESS

Everyone has a different definition of success. The purpose of this book, however, is to guide you towards realising and achieving your own version of success, by using this simple, clear pathway to gain control in this very fast-paced world.

Over the years, I've worked with CEOs, business owners, elite athletes, millionaires and celebrities, steering them all through this same process that you're about to embark on. A high-achieving bunch accustomed to massive success in their respective fields, they usually have one thing in common.

They crave to go back to the basics of their foundation to gain control, clarity and purpose so they can make small changes that will assist them in reaching their potential. Taking a snapshot of their life can often provide all the answers they need to make better decisions in everyday life.

Success is about self-management, which is your ability to motivate yourself and optimally leverage your own skills, experience and value in any direction you choose.

You don't need to make massive changes to achieve success in all areas of your life. It doesn't take a dramatic shift to your mindset or a brand new way of approaching your life to accomplish everything you want. Rather, it takes small consistent commitment to the blocks in your foundation, each with their own huge ripple effect — that can make the biggest impact.

This book gives you the tools to create a simple snapshot of your life, and shows you how to then establish a structure and path to support your visions, reminding you to be grateful along the way — and to acknowledge yourself and your achievements. It's a guide and step-by-step process to achieving a healthy, balanced and successful life.

"Success is neither magical nor mysterious.
Success is the natural consequence
of consistently applying the basic
fundamentals."

– Jim Rohn

START

the foundation of you

THE FOUNDATION OF YOU

Starting with a snapshot of you and where you're at in your life sets up the foundation for you to build and move forward with confidence. It's a simple fact-finding mission about the brand named 'you' and is the first step to self-management for success.

The first step begins with a simple question: 'Who are you?' It's one of the first questions I ask every new client and, the incredible thing is, most of them can't answer it.

You can answer however you like, but there's one caveat, and this is where most people come unstuck: you can't turn to the security of what you do to inform your response.

At the end of the day, you may be a CEO, an entrepreneur, an executive or a creative artist, but while this is what you *do*, it's not who you *are*.

Parent, employee, boss, landlord, partner, husband, wife, investor, client, friend, sister, uncle, business owner, soccer coach, coffee aficionado — these are all examples of the many different hats we wear in our everyday lives. These are the roles we play, rather than being a representation of who we are at the very core. Finding out exactly who the person is who performs all of these tasks and roles is liberating!

The question is actually less, 'Who am I?' and more, 'Who am I without my job, partner, career, home, car, hobbies, kids and family? What is at my core?'

QUESTIONS TO DISCOVER YOU

Asking yourself questions is one of the most powerful ways you can take control of what you want to achieve in life.

The answers lie within you and the means of seeking them out can strengthen your self-esteem and build your confidence. They also give you clarity, and cut through the fog and overload in your mind. They simplify the picture about who you are and what you're trying to do.

These questions will help you get started on the process of clearly defining who you are. Take sufficient time to answer each question fully and authentically, as they provide the framework on which you establish your values.

1. Who/what is most important to you?
2. Who/what are you inspired by?
3. What are you afraid of?
4. What are you putting up with right now?
5. How do you want to be remembered by your family?
6. What do you really want?

SNAPSHOTS
Start a book titled ME, where you record snapshots of each year and the answers to these questions.

CASE STUDY
Jack, CEO, national retail chain
Jack plays many roles, but underneath it all he is a person who values his past achievements, his health and who he is for his family. He has a vision and a plan to build his future that he is responsible for. He is committed to mindful living, listening and positive communication, all in the pursuit of fuelling his need to feel a sense of achievement in life.

OWN YOUR ACHIEVEMENTS

Achievement is the act of accomplishment or completion. It's something accomplished successfully, especially by means of exertion, skill, practice or perseverance...

Most of us are so busy churning along on the treadmill of everyday life that we tend to gloss over our achievements.

You'll often celebrate positive experiences, such as achieving a promotion, a sale or a home renovation with friends, relatives or colleagues at that present moment. Once the flowers have wilted and the champagne flutes are back in the cupboard, it's business as usual. Life goes on.

When you take the opportunity to remember and own your proudest moments, you become more aware and confident. That's why celebrating your successes on a routine basis is crucial: it allows you to regularly build your confidence and keep moving forward with both a positive mindset and a renewed motivation.

One quick, easy way to build this process of review into your routine is to book one hour per month in your diary as a 'review hour'. Allow yourself this hour to write down what you've accomplished throughout the month. This is the time to reflect, record and plan — it keeps your motivation going and ensures you're honest about how you've really been spending your time.

CASE STUDY
Acknowledgement to confidence
"It wasn't until I stopped and actually answered these questions that I realised, really acknowledged, where my life was at," admits George, who launched his own online marketing business in 2006. "Right now, I have the business and the lifestyle that from five or six years ago I was working so hard to achieve. It was uplifting to remember where I came from and just how much I've achieved and that, actually, this is exactly where I want to be!"

RECORD YOUR LIFE ACCOMPLISHMENTS

Be proud of what you've done, rather than constantly focusing on what you haven't done, and your attitude and motivation will shift. Sit and write a list of all the things you're proud of in your life.

1. What are three important things you've accomplished during your career and life?
2. What lessons have you learnt while accomplishing these things?
3. What are your skills and talents?
4. What do you do easily and effortlessly?
5. What made you happiest as a child, and are you still doing part of that?

"In the end, it's not going to matter how many breaths you took, but how many moments took your breath away."

– Shing Xiong

BEING MINDFUL

The art now is not just to look back and appreciate, but to live today as it happens. This is called 'mindful living'. To be mindful means to dwell deeply in the present moment, to be aware of what's going on within and around us. This promotes perspective in our chaotic world.

MY MAJOR ACHIEVEMENTS

- I've been truly honest with myself.
- I've taken responsibility for myself and my marriage, business, health, wealth and lifestyle.
- I've raised healthy, happy children.
- I've built an inspiring business, which has grown each and every year into a more successful and rewarding venture.
- I've overcome the debilitation of chronic fatigue.
- I've learnt the art of living with purpose and being 'in the moment'.

Book two 'special dinners' per year; this provides neutral ground and space to sit, reflect and acknowledge what you just achieved and how you got there. These provide motivation to keep wanting to achieve. They're a special highlight on my calendar!

YOUR GOLDEN MOMENTS

There is gold around you all the time if you choose to look at it, engage and be present. This is what gives depth to our lives. These are tiny snapshots for you to take daily; they're to be cherished and archived in your mind forever.

- Being promoted or offered a new job.
- Noticing the first blossom on a tree.
- The moment you find out you're having a baby.
- Walking out of an interview or meeting, and knowing you've nailed it.
- Seeing the bright lights of Times Square or Tokyo for the first time.
- Feeling the sand between your toes on a relaxing beach holiday.
- The glory of fireworks.
- The smell of a newspaper.
- The shape of water as it drips down a window.
- Catching a glance of your partner when they're daydreaming.
- Seeing a perfectly formed daisy.
- The first taste of chocolate in your mouth.
- Hearing your child giggle for the first time.
- Getting your licence and driving a car by yourself.
- Smelling fresh herbs or freshly cut grass.
- The smell of good coffee, or the taste of toast dripping in butter.
- Passing a test or exam with flying colours.

"To live is to choose. But to choose well, you must know who you are and what you stand for, where you want to go and why you want to get there."

– Kofi Annan

YOUR VALUES — THE KEY TO YOU

Defining your values is the first major step in unlocking your key to success. Once you've got them identified, it kicks off the process towards unlocking a great life. By letting your values guide and shape your priorities and reactions, you'll start to make decisions and take opportunities that are in line with your values — which will have the flow-on effect of leaving you feeling more content, happy and satisfied.

Consider whether or not you're living by your values.

Values are those things that really matter to you — the ideas and beliefs that you deem to be most important. Your own value system has likely been influenced by a range of factors, including your background, events that have happened or you have witnessed, your upbringing, your spiritual beliefs and your philosophy of life.

By making a deliberate and conscious effort to identify and live according to your key values, you can minimise the stress and anxiety in all areas of your life.

"Values are not just words, values are what we live by."

— John Kerry

MY TOP 3 VALUES

My top three values are **health** (both physical and mental), **family happiness** and who I am to my family, and having a sense of **achievement** daily. Understanding my values brings absolute clarity to every decision I make.

The characteristics I want to project are calm, confident and fun. My body is about strength and preservation, my travel is with purpose, my marriage is fun and inspirational, and my business is ever evolving.

In the past, my sense of achievement was always focused on doing more, being more efficient and more productive, and succeeding in business and sport. However, it's evolved to include the more nourishing tones of space, valuing the downtime just as much as the high-octane time, and realising that even doing the simple chores are achievements.

Values have a major influence on your behaviour and serve as broad guidelines in all situations. It's when your actions aren't in alignment with your values that you find yourself without a sense of achievement or feeling out of control.

CLARITY OF PURPOSE

THE VALUES GAME

Step 1: Select
Identify your top 10 values from the box of 30 to the right. Don't spend much time agonising over your decisions and go with your gut instinct.

Step 2: Prioritise
Prioritise each value from one to 10. Focus on your top five values and briefly define what each one means to you.

Step 3: Contemplate
Read each value slowly, letting the meaning of each word sink in so you fully understand what each one means to you.

Step 4: Define
Select your top three values and write them down. Memorise these, as they'll act as your decision-making blueprint from hereon in. You also need to define the single value that's the most important to you.

Step 5: Commit
Work out what you need to add or remove from your life, and what you need to change, to reflect these values.

FAMILY HAPPINESS (quality time, bonding)	SELF-RESPECT (sense of personal identity, pride)	GENEROSITY (helping others, improving society)
COMPETITIVENESS (winning, taking risks)	RECOGNITION (acknowledgement, status)	WISDOM (discovering and understanding knowledge)
FRIENDSHIP (close relationships with others)	ADVANCEMENT (promotions)	SPIRITUALITY (strong religious, spiritual beliefs)
AFFECTION (love, caring)	HEALTH (mental and physical)	LOYALTY (devotion, trustworthiness)
COOPERATION (working well with others, teamwork)	RESPONSIBILITY (being accountable for results)	CULTURE (race or ethnic identity)
ADVENTURE (new challenges)	FAME (public recognition)	INNER HARMONY (being at peace)
ACHIEVEMENT (a sense of accomplishment)	INVOLVEMENT (belonging, being involved with others)	ORDER (stability, conformity, tranquillity)
WEALTH (getting rich, making money)	ECONOMIC SECURITY (strong, consistent income streams)	CREATIVITY (being imaginative, innovative)
ENERGY (vitality, vim and vigour)	PLEASURE (fun, laughter, a leisurely lifestyle)	INTEGRITY (honesty, sincerity, standing up for oneself)
FREEDOM (independence and autonomy)	POWER (control, authority or influence over others)	PERSONAL DEVELOPMENT (use of personal potential)

"When you were born, you cried and the world rejoiced. Live your life so that when you die, the world cries and you rejoice."

– Cherokee Expression

YOUR GREATEST LESSONS LEARNT

What have been your greatest life lessons so far? The purpose of asking yourself this question is not to delve into an introspective review of lessons from the past. Rather, it's so you don't keep making the same mistakes, and thus you can grow, evolve and continue to learn.

Your greatest lessons help to shape you into the person you are, and despite the adversity you may face at the time, they ultimately make life more enjoyable and rewarding. For instance, after suffering from chronic fatigue syndrome due to being an overachiever, I've learnt that each time I say yes to anything, whether it's a job, an opportunity, a favour or an invitation, there's a cost involved. So, I need to be aware of that cost, whether it's my health, family time, or money, before I say yes.

The world's greatest leaders and business titans not only strive to learn from mistakes made in the past, but they take this task quite seriously, because they know how valuable it is for growth — both personal and professional — and your ability to move forward.

"Be thankful for what you have; you'll end up having more. If you concentrate on what you don't have, you will never, ever have enough."

– Oprah Winfrey

"The biggest obstacle to creating a wonderful life is self-limiting beliefs. A self-limiting belief is an idea you have that you're limited in some way, in terms of time, talent, intelligence, money, ability or opportunity."

— Brian Tracy

YOUR LIMITING BELIEFS

We all have beliefs about the world and the way we think it works. Through your individual experiences in life, without even realising it, you've established notions about what is — and isn't — possible and what you're capable of achieving.

Your beliefs, both positive and negative, profoundly affect every decision you make in life. For instance, procrastination can be caused by a limiting belief, as it confines you to your comfortable rut and protects you from whatever you might be afraid of.

- You're afraid of success.
- You're afraid of failure.
- You're afraid of what people will think or say.
- You're afraid of how people will treat you.
- You're afraid of change.
- You're afraid of making a mistake.
- You're afraid of being rejected.
- You're afraid you won't live up to other people's expectations.

"What you believe is what you achieve. You become what you affirm: positively affirm your greatness, genius and fullest potential."

– Mark Victor Hansen

HOW TO CONQUER LIMITING BELIEFS

Step 1: Expose
Expose your own negative beliefs when you catch yourself saying things such as, "I'm always unlucky with..." or "I can't do this because..."

Step 2: Record
Identify and record your negative beliefs when you become aware of them, then read them aloud.

Step 3: Affirm
Affirm and repeat the belief that is *opposite* to your limiting belief.

Step 4: Find proof
You believe something to be true because the facts seem to support it, so open your mind and search for the facts that deny it.

Step 5: Be responsible
Choose your own beliefs and the way you want to live and behave.

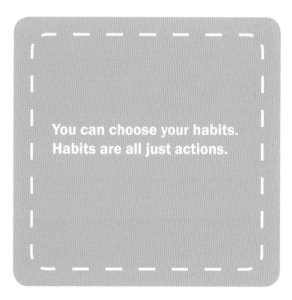

You can choose your habits.
Habits are all just actions.

WHO AM I?

- I'm your constant companion.
- I'm your greatest helper and heaviest burden.
- I'll push you onward or drag you down to failure.

- I'm completely at your command.
- Half the things you do, you might as well turn over to me and I'll be able to do them quickly and correctly.
- I'm easily managed — you must merely be firm with me.

- Show me exactly how you want something done and after a few lessons, I'll do it automatically.
- I'm the servant of all great men and women, but alas, of all failures as well.
- Those who are great, I've made great. Those who are failures, I've made failures.

- I'm not a machine, though I work with all the precision of a machine, plus the intelligence of a woman or a man.
- You may run me for profit or ruin — it makes no difference to me.
- Take me, train me, be firm with me, and I'll place the world at your feet.
- Be easy with me and I'll destroy you.

  Answer: I am your habits. - Anonymous

Tom's ticket to freedom — understanding his values

Just as Tom discovered, the secret is to never forget to address the basics...

Tom is a small business owner and a client of mine. In a nutshell, when we met, he was overworked, exhausted, and had no delegation or time management skills.

Financially, he was successful. Tom's bank balance wasn't only healthy, but swelling at a rate he only dreamed about when he dared to "quit the rat race" to launch his own enterprise.

He initially launched his business so he'd have more flexibility in his life. With no boss to answer to, he planned to spend more time with his wife and kids, and gain a better work-life balance.

Instead, he was working longer hours than ever before and seeing his family less and less, which had the flow-on effect of creating tension in his marriage, not to mention his lack of health management and poor fitness levels.

The dilemma

- Tom's main problem was that he wasn't making any decisions based on his core values.
- His number one value was his family, and yet his marriage was unhappy.
- Business was strong, so Tom ploughed all of his energy into work, clocking up 70 to 80 hours across six to seven days a week.
- As a result, Tom rarely saw his wife and kids, which made him feel guilty, but he also felt pressure to work hard and build a financially secure future.
- Tom felt ungrateful for complaining about having too much work when others in his industry were struggling to stay afloat, but he acknowledged that he needed to slow down, add emotion at home and become relevant to his family.

The solution

- Tom defined his working hours and cut back on his time spent at the office, so he had to be more productive and organised.
- He dedicated 6pm to 8pm every night for special family time.
- Every second Saturday night, Tom organised a babysitter so he could have time with his wife.
- He covered his home and office with Post-it notes to remind himself of his new journey and to gain clarity.
- Tom also redefined his idea of success, as he realised it meant nothing more than to be respected by himself, his family, peers and clients.

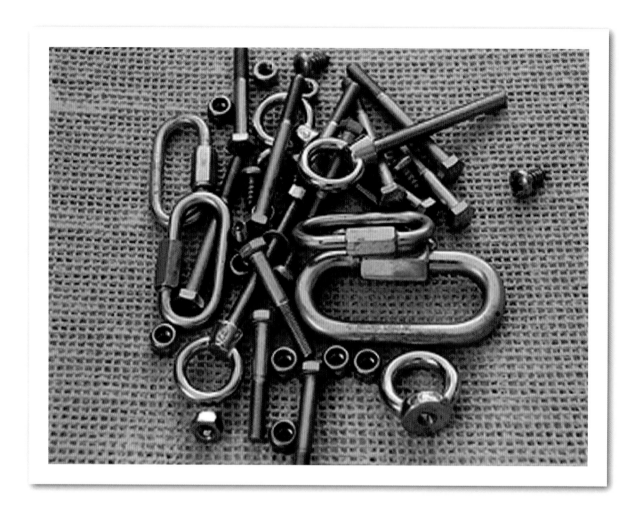

"They say the chains of habit are too light to be felt until they're too heavy to be broken. The chains you put around yourself now have enormous consequences as you go through life."

– Warren Buffett

THE FOUNDATION FOR SUCCESS

Remember:
- Always go back to the basics.
- Take note of the golden moments.
- Be aware of your values when making decisions.
- Own your limiting beliefs and work to reduce them.
- Above all, a shift in attitude can mean a shift in life.

MY NOTES

_____

_____

_____

_____

_____

_____

_____

_____

_____

_____

_____

_____

_____

_____

_____

_____

_____

"Life is really simple, but we insist on making it complicated."

– Confucius

SIMPLIFY

"That's been one of my mantras: focus and simplicity. Simple can be harder than complex: you have to work hard to get your thinking clean to make it simple. But it's worth it in the end because once you get there, you can move mountains."

– Steve Jobs

"I run my best when I'm happy and relaxed. I need balance and stability in my life in order to do this. Shannah has helped me to simplify my life and create this balance, which I so much needed, but didn't quite know where to start..."

— Benita Willis, Olympian and Australian marathon record holder

SIMPLIFY

Simplicity is one of the most valuable and yet most underrated qualities you can strive to embrace in your life. Simplicity represents clarity, presence and freedom from effort. When you simplify your life, you effectively clear your mind so you can continue on your journey with confidence and motivation.

After exploring the first section of the book, you now have clarity on your values, what you've achieved in your life and what you're proud of. You've realised that your habits and attitude determine most of your success, and you've become acquainted with your limiting beliefs.

The next step is to become clear on exactly what you want to achieve and how you want your life to look, so you can grab on to the right opportunities when life presents them.

Before you start reaching for your goals, you need to get back to basics. This means clearing the clutter, deleting the drainers and getting clarity in all areas, so you can build a structure to support your best possible life.

SIMPLICITY = CLARITY

1. Clarity reduces ambiguity and eliminates doubt.
2. When you simplify your life, you emerge from the fog and can move forward with a clear head.
3. You then have the space and opportunity to set purposeful goals that match your vision for your future.

YOUR ENERGY DRAINERS

Decluttering your life is the next step towards creating a simpler, more streamlined environment. This is the big clean-out you'll need to do before you can structure new opportunities and strategies that support you to be your best, with optimal wellness both personally and professionally.

High achievers often struggle with feeling cluttered, overwhelmed and overextended because they take on so much of everything and create a great amount of opportunity! Working parents also know only too well how difficult it is to juggle work, life and play.

No one is immune to the burden of being mentally cluttered. The barista at your local coffee shop may be chatting politely as he foams your latte, but he's also wondering whether he should move in with his girlfriend, thinking about his dinner plans, working out whether he can afford to go skiing next month... and don't those concert tickets go on sale tomorrow?

WHAT'S DRAINING YOU?

Many people are surprised to realise how much satisfaction can be derived from small, seemingly inconsequential tasks, such as putting all of your gadget chargers in one place, booking a check-up with the dentist or filing all of your documents in their correct folders.

These types of tasks may not seem like a big priority on the surface, but they can absorb mental space and chip away at your everyday focus.

By making small tweaks to your routine, you can create space within your life to manage and create everything you want to achieve. Clearing your drainers doesn't only have a massive positive impact on your energy, but also your confidence, as you'll experience the satisfaction of accomplishment — remembering to celebrate all of the wins, big and small — on a regular basis.

- Drainers are like tiny sandbags that are stacked at the back of your neck.

- Each sandbag on its own may be small and insignificant, but combined, they weigh us down and make us feel tired and lethargic.

- Your personal environment, finances, relationships and wellbeing are the key areas where you need to simplify and eliminate drainers.

IDENTIFY YOUR DRAINERS

Drainers aren't things you think about consciously, but are tasks that are in your subconscious. The more you focus on these basics, the simpler your life will be.

Personal environment

1. Is your living space clean and inspiring? ☐
2. Is your wardrobe tidy and are all of your clothes clean, pressed and in good repair? ☐
3. Have you cleaned out all of your storage space and thrown away anything you haven't used in two years? ☐
4. Do you have fresh air and comfort in your home? ☐
5. Is your bed, pillow and bedding clean, comfortable and conducive to a good night's sleep? ☐

Relationships

1. Do you let the people you love know how important they are to you? ☐
2. Do you tidy any loose ends with your partner, parents, siblings and friends by having open, honest and authentic conversations? ☐
3. Have you let go of any relationships that drag you down or damage you? ☐
4. Do you give your partner and family quality time, or are you taking action to meet a partner if you're single? ☐
5. Do you respond to all phone calls, letters and emails promptly, even if your response is brief? ☐

Wellbeing

1. Does your diet include fresh fruit and vegetables, and provide you with energy? □
2. Do you avoid excess tea, coffee and alcohol? □
3. Do you exercise for 30 minutes at least three times per week? □
4. Do you get enough sleep at least five nights out of seven? □
5. Do you have a holiday at least once a year? □

Finances

1. Do you have a budget? □
2. Do you pay your bills on time or make arrangements with creditors? □
3. Are all of your receipts, invoices and financial records filed and in order? □
4. Do you have an automatic savings plan to save at least 10% of your income? □
5. Do you pay off your credit card debt in full monthly? □

Fun/creativity

1. Do you invest in personal development? □
2. Do you laugh every day? □
3. Do you have a hobby? □
4. Do you plan regular fun activities with your partner, family and friends? □
5. Do you dream big and believe that nothing's impossible? □

"Taking the time to identify my values and better understand the aspects of my life that were draining me has allowed me to move forward with a much clearer perspective, and greater clarity around my personal and career goals."

– Director, PricewaterhouseCoopers Australia

"Clutter is stuck energy. The word 'clutter' derives from the Middle English word 'clotter', which means to coagulate and that's about as stuck as you can get."

– Karen Kingston

3 QUICK CLUTTER FIXES

1. Make simple requests of others.
2. Have a clean environment.
3. Know your finances.

HOW TO STAY CLUTTER-FREE

- Review your list of drainers monthly.
- Aim to move each answer from "no" to "yes".
- Diarise time to maintain your personal environment, finances, relationships and wellbeing.
- Create a system to achieve all of the tasks you've set yourself to clear the drainers from your life.

CASE STUDY

Lisa has a senior position within a large fashion brand and although successful, she often felt angry, overworked and out of control. She decided to take responsibility for her life. She put the word SIMPLIFY up in her home and every day her goal was to simplify just one thing. She created a structure to support more joyful pursuits by booking fun dates and exercise into her diary.

Lisa mapped out the year ahead, booking in quarterly holidays and planning restful weekends away with her husband every eight weeks. She created a timeline with clarity and simplicity that kept her motivated and inspired to keep moving forward.

"Balance is not better time management, but better boundary management. Balance means making choices and enjoying those choices."

- Betsy Jacobson

YOUR BOUNDARIES

If you feel overwhelmed with too much on your plate and not enough time to do it, buffers and boundaries will set you free.

But boundaries aren't just useful for those who overload their schedule or have trouble saying "no". Both at work and at play, boundaries provide a valuable structure to communicate with those around you so that everyone achieves their desired outcome without feeling frustrated or resentful.

To create a more balanced life, the key is to set boundaries that support your visions, goals and the way you function at your best. But first, you need to know where your boundaries are...

> Use your smart phone to help you simplify and declutter your mental space. Do this by programming alerts to take your multivitamins or medication at the same time each morning, or prompts every couple of hours to drink water, stand up and stretch your legs. It keeps the important tasks simple for you and covers the basics without you having to remember it all.

CASE STUDY: Boundaries at work

Martin was able to complete his most important tasks in the morning, so he didn't mind making himself more available to his colleagues in the afternoon. To achieve this outcome, he always started with the hardest task first. He also set the boundary that when his office door was closed, his colleagues weren't allowed to enter unless their request was urgent, and if it was open, they had to knock before entering.

CASE STUDY: Boundaries at home

Darcy realised that his partner and family were the most important people in his life. Between 6pm and 9pm each evening, he decided to engage with them, and did so by not checking his phone or emails during this time. He also consciously opened the front door each evening with a smile and positive energy, to inspire rather than drain his family. Darcy changed his family dynamic by making these commitments.

CASE STUDY: Boundaries for yourself

By making one basic health commitment to yourself, such as giving up or limiting alcohol or coffee, you can bring about a huge positive change. Jenny lost 4kg in six months by simply giving up soft drink.

YOUR CHARACTERISTICS

High achievers possess certain characteristics that are integral to success. Characteristics are personality traits, not skills, that can be learnt and cultivated just like any other skill set. They're often the most important and effective.

Consider the experience of an elite athlete, such as a world champion swimmer. They obviously have advanced skills in their chosen sport, but they weren't born that way. They worked hard to develop their skills and hone their craft, because they possessed certain characteristics — drive, determination, passion, persistence — that forced them to get up at 4am each morning to train for six hours per day, six days a week.

Whatever your goals in life, if you develop the characteristics of an ambitious person, you'll make progress towards your outcomes and you'll succeed.

Sometimes the answer to success is identifying the simple characteristic that's needed.

"You cannot dream yourself into a
character; you must hammer and
forge yourself into one."

– Henry David Thoreau

WHAT'S YOUR OPPORTUNITY?

If you're struggling with a certain situation or trait, evaluate it against this list and you'll find your answer. When you unlock this piece of the puzzle, you'll identify exactly which small changes you can make for the biggest impact.

In going through this process, Olympic runner Benita Willis realised that although it was her passion, running had taken over her life. She ran too much and had lost her love for it. She had no vision for her life outside of sport, so she built a new routine that supported a full, inspiring, balanced lifestyle that was separate to her running. "I never believed I could achieve so much while being an elite athlete!" she says. "I feel confident in all areas of my life now and look forward to an exciting future — as an athlete and beyond."

WINNER'S LIST: 11 CHARACTERISTICS OF SUCCESS

1. They have a vision — one that's whole, inspiring, balanced and exciting.

2. They have a plan — one that's well thought out to back up their vision.

3. They work hard — high-level success starts with the recognition that hard work pays off.

4. They have knowledge or training — and they're committed to adapting and growing continually to improve their skills.

5. They're eager to learn — winners study, ask questions, read and research, and then apply what they learn.

6. They're persistent — where many people stop at the first rejection, they look for other opportunities to reach their outcome.

7. They take responsibility for their actions — because they know that when they blame, they disempower themselves.

8. They network — because they value people and relationships and have contact lists full of people who value their friendship.

9. They make decisions — where most people procrastinate.

10. They're self-reliant — they take initiative and accept the responsibilities of success.

11. They live in the present moment — successful people don't waste time, they use it and are mindful with their tasks.

YOUR VISION

Having a vision for your future can be a very powerful, motivating force. By crafting a clear vision and purpose, you can effectively communicate your intentions and motivate yourself towards an inspiring picture of the future.

For long-term success, creating a vision and purpose is critical. Without it, you're a passenger — and to get in the driver's seat in order to actively work towards achieving your goals, you need to know where you're going.

"A vision is not just a picture of what could be; it is an appeal to our better selves, a call to become something more."

– Rosabeth Moss Kanter

8 VISION CREATION THOUGHT STARTERS

1. What do I want to see in my travels?
2. What am I passionate about in life?
3. What type of person do I want to become?
4. What do I want to have and achieve?
5. What hobbies have I developed/do I want to develop so I'm great at them and enjoy them with depth and achievement?
6. What would I like to share?
7. How do I want to inspire others?
8. What have I conquered financially and emotionally?

CREATING YOUR VISION

Step 1

Write a vision and purpose statement of where you'd like to be in three years' time. Consider your age at that point and you'll get an instant visual to help with your answers.

Tips
- Use 'what', 'who', 'when' and 'how' to bring your vision to life.
- Write in the present tense, as if you're living that dream.
- Don't let lack of money, skills or time be a barrier.
- Don't think of what you can do at the moment, but what you'd ultimately love to do.
- Put aside any limitations and create the dream life for yourself.
- Describe how you feel in the new vision.

Beware of dream stealers: those people who encourage you to play it safe and make you believe you'll never reach your dreams. Who are your dream stealers?

CASE STUDY: Jack's vision

"I'm relaxing at a five-star resort in Thailand with my family, enjoying the fruits of success from a very committed year of work. I'm on a career high after landing a very prestigious and lucrative promotion, which I've been working towards my entire career, and I feel creatively satisfied in my work. We own a beautiful home on the water, which we're renovating, and we've just settled on our second investment property purchase. We're planning a two-month family adventure around Europe next year. My wife and I also enjoy fortnightly 'date nights' and weekend getaways without the kids every three to four months. I've spent the past couple of years working on my self-development as a person, and I feel happy and content with who I am, both personally and professionally. It's liberating to experience such freedom as a result of planning who I am and where I want to get to..."

Step 2

Talk to others about your dreams and desires. This is fundamental in helping bring them to life.

Step 3

Detail your vision by cutting it down into sizeable goals that are achievable, as they have a structure to support them.

Tips
- Work out exactly what you need to help you achieve your vision.
- Plan how you're going to achieve your vision.
- Construct a timeline outlining when you're going to achieve your vision including the smaller steps along the way.

Step 4

Create a visual document of your vision. This is a collage of all the things you'd like to have, do or become.

Tips:
- Make a list of your goals and think about how you can translate this goal visually into an image.
- Include beautiful pictures and words that inspire you.
- Focus on different areas of your life, including relationships, health, wealth, family and spirituality.
- Choose motivators that remind you to develop, evolve, flourish and stay a little challenged.

Step 5

Journal your gratitude along the way and celebrate all of the steps, both big and small, that take you closer to your goals. University of California psychologist Robert Emmons states that gratitude should be thought of as a discipline or skill, akin to goal setting or time management.

"The greater danger for most of us lies not in setting our aim too high and falling short; but in setting our aim too low, and achieving our mark."

— Michelangelo

Gratitude

YOUR GOALS

When setting goals, you're ultimately deciding what's next in your life, so you can strategise how to get it. Goals initiate behaviours and consequences maintain behaviours. So when you set simple, achievable goals with a time frame, accountability and support, you'll succeed.

The more detailed you are with your ambitions, the more motivated you'll be as you get closer to achieving them. This means using tangible words in your goals, including measurements and time frames. Rather than thinking "I'll get a promotion", be more specific: "I'll be promoted to senior executive by the end of next year, with a 15% pay rise."

If you're serious about achieving your aims, they must be written down. This was proven in a U.S. study*, which found that people who wrote their goals down accomplished significantly more than those who didn't. The positive effect of accountability was also supported: those who sent weekly progress reports to a colleague or friend achieved much more than those who had unwritten goals, or who simply wrote them down without making themselves accountable.

*Summary of Recent Goals Research, Gail Matthews, Ph.D., Dominican University

5 STEPS TO CLARIFY YOUR GOALS

1. What are your goals in simple terms?
2. Are you clear on your specific objectives?
3. Why are you doing this?
4. What do you really want to achieve?
5. Do your goals have depth and do you really understand them?

IDENTIFY YOUR TOP 3 GOALS

- Carry them with you all day.
- Program them into your phone.
- Write them on a card and store them in your wallet.
- Copy them into your diary or planner to greet you when you open the front page each day.

"Develop an attitude of gratitude, and give thanks for everything that happens to you, knowing that every step forward is a step toward achieving something bigger and better than your current situation."

– Brian Tracy

When setting your goals, start with the big picture. When you begin with your end vision, including those big dreams and lofty, pie-in-the-sky ambitions, you can work out how to break them down into smaller wins, where each step takes you closer to your end goal.

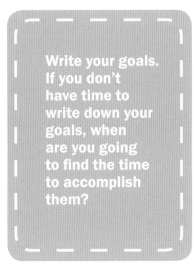

Write your goals. If you don't have time to write down your goals, when are you going to find the time to accomplish them?

3 GOALS
I wish to achieve this year

....
....
....
....
....
....
....
....
....
....
....
....
....
....

SHANNAH KENNEDY

"The victory of success is half won when one gains the habit of setting goals and achieving them. Even the most tedious chore will become endurable as you parade through each day convinced that every task, no matter how menial or boring, brings you closer to fulfilling your dreams."

– Og Mandino

MY NOTES

_____

_____

_____

_____

_____

_____

_____

_____

_____

_____

_____

_____

_____

_____

_____

_____

_____

"If you fail to plan, you plan to fail."
– Benjamin Franklin

STRUCTURE

STRUCTURE

The foundations are set, the clutter is gone, you have simplicity in what you want out of life and you know what you need to do to get there. It's time to compile and use the tools in this chapter to plan how you operate and build your vision for optimal living.

It may sound obvious, but creating routine and structure in your day is the key to creating a calm, balanced and successful life. Structure is a powerful and highly underrated tool that will *fundamentally change your life* for the better.

To achieve your goals, every part of your life needs to be planned for and supported. And I mean *everything*: work, exercise, nutrition, money, fun, time out — every activity and every element in your life needs to be supported.

When you have the right structure in place, you have the freedom to be spontaneous and to grab new opportunities without sacrificing any of your obligations. It gives you balance, clarity and, just as importantly, the space to work towards achieving your ambitions.

"Your time is limited, so don't waste it living someone else's life."

— Steve Jobs

TIME MANAGEMENT IS SELF-MANAGEMENT

Some people — in fact, I'd hazard a guess that *most* people — spend more time planning their annual holiday than they do planning their life as a whole.

Those few weeks spent 'checking out' of daily life are planned, analysed, reviewed, shared and added to the calendar in big, bold letters as something to look forward to. There's nothing wrong with looking forward to a holiday, but it becomes a problem when it's viewed as all a person really has to live for each year!

It's important to value time and to understand what it's doing for you — not just when you're taking a break, but in each and every moment. How you structure your activities will either give you a sense of achievement, fulfilment, energy and success, or it will make you feel stressed, out of control and exhausted.

Time is a gift and it's our responsibility to really own and drive our time and what we want to do with it. This means taking ownership of what we want to feel (calm, unhurried and relaxed — or rushed, anxious and stressed), and understanding the consequences of each of our activities.

Check your perception of time. Time can be too fast and sometimes just too slow. Your perception of time also changes, depending on your circumstances. Ask any woman in the throes of labour, and she'll tell you that one minute is a *very* long time! Consider how a 15-minute unit of time feels when you're in the following situations:

- On a freeway in bumper-to-bumper traffic.
- Sipping cocktails on a relaxing vacation.
- Running late for an appointment or meeting.
- Someone is running late for an appointment with you.
- At the beginning of a fun one-hour lunch date.
- In a long queue at the bank, post office or supermarket.
- At the airport when your flight is delayed.

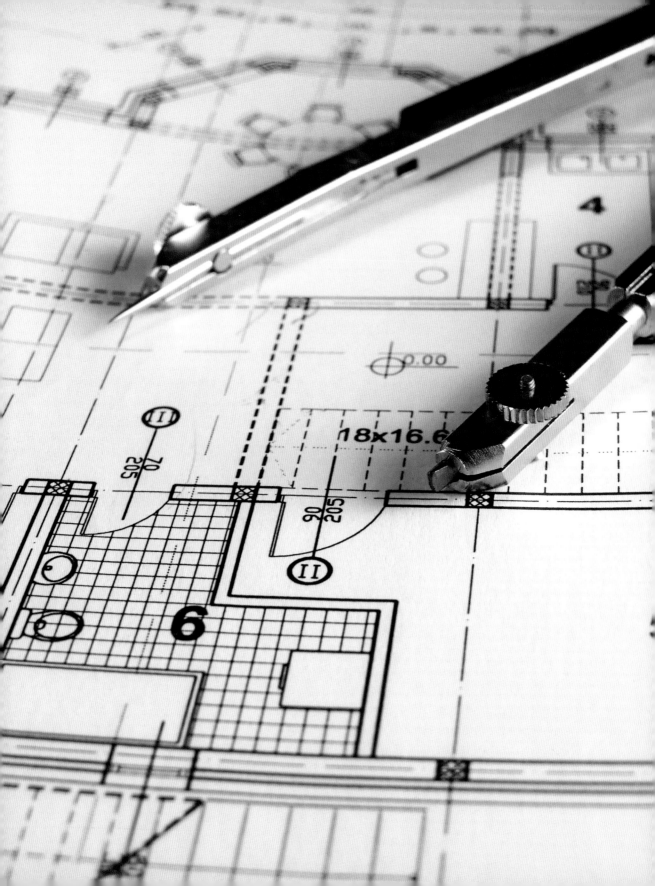

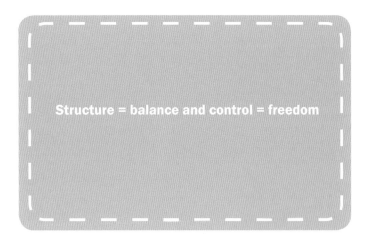

Structure = balance and control = freedom

TIME TOOL #1: DIARY/DAY PLANNER

"My life is so hectic," people complain. "I'm rushing from one thing to the next; I'm always busy. I've got so much on my plate and I never have any time for myself." More often than not it's these same people who say they don't have a diary or a planner that is used efficiently.

It's *impossible* to have control over your life if you have no structure to support your daily activities, which means you must have a diary or a planner.

Not having a diary is an act of self-sabotage. It's like charging expenses on your credit card all month and not keeping tabs on your spending, never asking for receipts, then complaining that your credit card bill is so high.

5 questions to guide your diary planning
1. Have I covered my values?
2. Have I booked in downtime to recharge?
3. Have I booked in quality time with those most important to me?
4. What are the rewards and consequences?
5. Have I structured balance by using my toolbox well?

You'll then see how much time you actually do have to be spontaneous!

Not having a diary is an
act of self-sabotage.

"Productivity is never an accident. It is always the result of a commitment to excellence, intelligent planning, and focused effort."

- Paul J. Meyer

TIME TOOL #2: MONTHLY AND YEARLY PLANNER

The world's most effective leaders understand that forward planning is essential for success. By loosely planning your month and year in advance, you'll not only be prepared for the busy times, but also incorporate regular milestones to look forward to.

Depth and fulfillment in life depends on how you value each and every moment. It's important to plan time so you can achieve, unwind and feel things — or life will go on without you.

Your planner acts as a framework to achieve this. A detailed monthly planner gives you the perspective and focus to move from the passenger side into the driver's seat.

Aim to update your monthly planner once a week. It takes only 10 minutes to sit down with your diary on one side and your monthly planner on the other, and transfer tasks and activities from one to the other. During each weekly update, tick off the things you've achieved — this will give you a sense of accomplishment, and thereby boost your confidence — and tweak upcoming events and activities to reflect any changes.

"Once you have mastered time, you will understand how true it is that most people overestimate what they can accomplish in a year - and underestimate what they can achieve in a decade!"

- Tony Robbins

5 STEPS TO GET INTO THE DRIVER'S SEAT

1. **Personal things get booked in first:** Book personal time in, as you would for a meeting. For example, your first hour at home each evening is your most important meeting of the day.
2. **Plan your health and wellbeing second:** Exercise, food, fun, mental breathing space and time out should be shaped around your work hours.
3. **Allow time for drainer-busting:** Carve out time to attack your to-do list. For example, update your finances, keep the house inspiring and spring clean every six months, service the car, get haircuts and spend one day every six months working on you.
4. **Delegate:** If there are things on your list that can be easily delegated, then delegate — there are no rewards for being a control freak!
5. **Breathe:** Take a deep breath and relax, knowing that now you don't have to think, as your critical list is taken care of — and you own it.

MY MONTHLY PLAN

1. **Health:** Exercise is booked in, including when I'll run, lift weights, stretch and go to yoga. Massages and listening to downloads are also booked in.
2. **Family:** Date nights, time with the kids, time with my extended family, and some fun time and dinners with friends are all booked in.
3. **Achievement:** This focuses on my work for the month — when is it best for me to have full coaching days, and what days are more suited to paperwork days or working on the business days?

Creating an annual planner from scratch may seem daunting initially, but you'll be surprised by how quickly and easily it can be filled. Start by inputting the 'fun' things, like birthdays, anniversaries, holidays, public holidays and social events, then add health and exercise, your drainers, career milestones and goals.

WORK GOALS

MAJOR WORK EVENTS

MARKETING
Photo shoot for catalogue
Costings for catalogue production

FINANCIALS
Conduct half year business reviews with direct reports
Reset business plan in line with required changes
Review weekly performance

PEOPLE
Birthdays — clients/staff
Newsletter — social media
Strategy dinner

CLIENTS
Specific client focus for month
Update product info
Forecasting
Marketing communication for the month

SAFETY
Recruit new OH&S Coordinator
Book Sydney workshop

CONFERENCES
Regional Conference Sydney
Industry Golf Day
Networking breakfast
BDM training session x2
PD day Perth

NETWORK
Coffee with Harry
Coffee with Nicole
Phone calls x6 new starts
Interview with BRW
Interview with The Age

JULY

PERSONAL GOALS

One session a week at the driving range
Photography group
Taste my food — be in the moment

FOCUS ON
Senses
Being present
Responsibility v blame

Weight 68kg
Target weight 67kg
Run x2 per week
Weights x1 per week
Stretching/yoga
Dentist

FOCUS ON
Body is temple
Water is key to energy level
8 hours sleep per night

OTHER

GENERAL
Date night
Update finances
Update monthly/yearly calendar
Clean out shed
Update photo albums
Windows cleaned
Car serviced

SOCIAL
Dinner with Mum/Dad
Dinner with Romy/Tim
Dinner with Carol
Lunch with Deb
Coffee with photography group

BIRTHDAYS
Mia 5th
Michael 19th
Kaye 21st
Jack 31st

REMEMBER
Responsibility v blame/ be present in the moment/ slow down/ enjoy the small stuff.

MOTTO FOR THE YEAR
I listen, I learn, I act, I'm accountable, I decide, I communicate, I plan, I laugh, I love, I'm affectionate, I enjoy. Attitude is my altitude.

GOAL OF THE MONTH
Complete all personal financials for new financial year.

RESPONSIBILITY VS BLAME

When many people hear the word 'responsibility', they immediately associate it with burden or having to carry a load. The sort of responsibility I'm referring to is the sort that leads to freedom.

When you take on the perspective that someone or something else has caused a situation, you choose to blame, which leaves you powerless and often resentful. When you take on the perspective that you may have contributed to cause a situation, you choose responsibility, which allows you to modify this situation with a sense of power and freedom.

Blame leads to disempowerment and loss of freedom.

Responsibility leads to freedom. Responsibility is asking, 'What have I done to cause or impact this? What can I now do about it?'

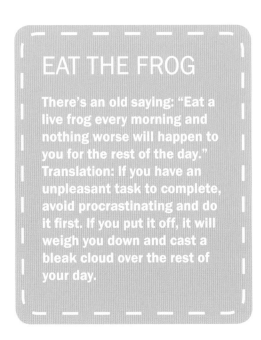

EAT THE FROG

There's an old saying: "Eat a live frog every morning and nothing worse will happen to you for the rest of the day." Translation: If you have an unpleasant task to complete, avoid procrastinating and do it first. If you put it off, it will weigh you down and cast a bleak cloud over the rest of your day.

CHOOSE TO BLAME = CHOOSE TO BURDEN

When you blame something or someone (including yourself) for any situation, you give away your power and put yourself in the position of being a victim. In other words, when you choose to blame, you choose *burden*.

By accepting that you're completely responsible for yourself, you choose freedom. There's very little that you can't achieve after you accept the notion that 'if it's to be, it's up to me'. The opposite of accepting responsibility is making excuses and allocating blame for what's going on in your life.

Consider Iain, a finance broker who, at the age of 55, lost a lot of money in share investments. He was angry. He felt cheated. He had watched a large amount of his life savings disappear and he blamed his financial adviser for giving him bad advice. He was becoming very bitter over the whole ordeal, which was holding him back from setting new financial goals for his retirement. He had agreed to make the investment, which was a gamble, and therefore needed to take responsibility for the situation.

As well as being disempowering, to blame is to dwell and an incredible waste of time. Once you understand the concept of responsibility, you're able to forgive yourself and others for mistakes and move forward.

4 STEPS TO GET YOUR LIFE MOVING

1. Think of three things that you're taking responsibility for in your life.
2. Now, think of three things for which you blame yourself or others.
3. What are the ways that you could have contributed to, or caused, the situation or result?
4. What can you do about it now in order to move forward and free up your time and energy?

COMMITMENT VS TRYING

When you're truly committed to your goals, you achieve them. Often, the problem isn't whether or not you're committed to achieving your outcome; the problem is that your level of commitment isn't high enough to really get things done.

As a human being, you're *always* committed to something — there's never a time where you aren't committed. Even when you're lying on the couch watching television, you may think you're not committed to anything, but in that scenario, you're committed to 'lying on the couch and watching television'. There's also the possibility that there's an even stronger underlying commitment...

UNDERLYING COMMITMENTS

Your underlying commitments are the unseen forces that drive your thoughts and beliefs and, as a consequence, your choices. They're responsible for that discrepancy between what you say you want to achieve and what you actually experience.

This was the case with Jennifer, a digital media consultant I coached, who had a goal to transform her small side business into a full-time job. She couldn't quite get it off the ground, until she realised that her underlying commitment was to financial security.

Growing up with a salesman father who lived on commissions, Jennifer knew how much pressure an inconsistent income had put on her family. She didn't want to risk losing her stable salary to work in her own business, with its potentially lucrative but unstable income stream, so she kept putting it off. Once she identified her limiting belief, Jennifer was able to put practical steps in place (including cutting back to part-time employment), so she could transition toward full-time business ownership without feeling stressed and financially insecure.

Underlying commitments can also have a positive and negative face. For example, being independent can be a wonderful thing, but it can also be a hindrance. It's about identifying what you're truly committed to and working with it for a positive outcome.

Get clarity on what you're truly committed to. Identify this and keep it simple so you can work with it regularly to achieve your best results.

DIFFERENT LEVELS OF COMMITMENT

Following through on commitments is very powerful. It builds your confidence and builds trust with everyone around you. Think of each task on your to-do list and consider where it fits on your scale of commitment. Has it been sitting there for months, waiting for you to find the time? What level of commitment are you operating at?

Every time you just 'try', instead of truly committing to achieving a set task, you rob yourself of time and energy (both physical and emotional). You then risk damaging your self-confidence when you don't achieve.

THE 5 LEVELS OF COMMITMENT

1. "Hmm…"
2. "I'll think about it."
3. "I'll do it (unless something comes up)."
4. "I'll do it unless I'm hit by a bus."
5. "I'll drag myself there bloodied and broken if I have to."

Martin says, "I'll try to quit smoking this weekend." What Martin really means is, "I'm not ready to commit to quitting smoking and I haven't fully explored the commitments that are fulfilled by my smoking. By using the word 'try', I can avoid quitting smoking and I can avoid exploring what my commitment to smoking means." This is a world away from, "I *will* stop smoking on Saturday."

COMMON SELF-SABOTAGES

- Fear of success.
- Fear of failure.
- Beliefs such as, "I'm not good enough," or "There isn't enough to go around."
- Beliefs such as, "I'm independent — I don't need help."
- Beliefs such as, "I don't deserve it."

THE KEY TO FULFILMENT

The key to living a successful, fulfilling life — as opposed to making excuses — is by getting in touch with your *real* reasons for not following through with your actions.

- Write down a goal or desire that you've been unable to attain. Eg. "Work out at the gym twice a week."

- Make a list of the actions you've taken (or not taken) that are in direct opposition to this goal. Eg. "Worked longer hours, so told myself I didn't have time; stopped working out with my gym buddy and lost that accountability; eventually cancelled gym membership as I wasn't using it."

- Imagine that these choices, which have taken you away from your desired goal, are an expression of a deeper commitment. Consider: "What commitment are these choices in direct alignment with?" Eg. "My gym membership is expensive and I'm not getting value, so I'll cancel it and save money."

- Now that you know the real reason why this underlying commitment has held you back, reset your goal and truly commit to it, today! Eg. "Sign up at an affordable gym that offers better value and classes that you really like; find a friend to work out with and re-establish motivation and accountability."

"What we think, or what we know, or what we believe, is of little consequence. The only consequence is what we do."

- John Ruskin

YOUR MOTIVATION

Wanting to do something and motivating yourself to actually do it are two very different things.

The distinction between those people who never reach their goals and those who achieve one goal after another, often comes down to their self-motivation.

This is your internal drive to achieve, produce, develop, evolve and essentially keep moving forward. When you think you're ready to give up or when you just don't know how to start, your self-motivation is what prompts you to go on.

Self-motivation is linked to your level of initiative in setting challenging goals for yourself, and your belief that you have the skills and abilities required to achieve your goals.

"Ability is what you're capable of doing.
Motivation determines what you do.
Attitude determines how well you do it."

– Lou Holtz

Four factors necessary to build the strongest levels of self-motivation:

1. **Confidence.** When you're confident, you're resilient and driven, and view difficult goals as being challenging rather than impossible. You're also more likely to bounce back from setbacks and believe in your ability to succeed.

2. **Positive thinking.** It's crucial to look at every situation positively, especially when things aren't going as planned or when unexpected setbacks arise. Think less, "I knew I couldn't do this," and more, "This one failure isn't going to stop me!"

3. **Focus.** Strong goals give you focus, a clear sense of direction, and the self-confidence that comes from recognising your own achievements.

4. **A motivating environment.** Surround yourself with supportive people and resources that remind you of your goals, and help you with your internal motivation.

YOUR SUPPORT

No one can achieve everything on their own. Build a support network of trustworthy people to help you reach your goals, both personally and professionally. Who's on your team? It could include coaches, mentors, books, network groups and exercise groups.

"People grow through experience
if they meet life honestly and
courageously. This is how character
is built."

– Eleanor Roosevelt

"The past, I think, has helped me appreciate the present – and I don't want to spoil any of it by fretting about the future."

– Audrey Hepburn

OPTIMAL LIVING

As much as this book talks about structure, planning and looking forward, being present and in the moment is an important life skill to practice and conquer.

By this stage, you know more about yourself than when you started the process. Building from your values, you know how to structure them into your daily life through your carefully designed planner, which takes into account every aspect of your life.

It's not just about being more organised, although that is a wonderful new benefit. The real purpose of harnessing these planning strategies is so you can stop fretting about getting everything done. Instead, you can relax in the knowledge that everything has been allocated its own time and space, allowing you the chance to enjoy and be present in your daily tasks.

Wherever you are — at home, on a plane, in a meeting — if you're fully present with your senses, you can really live life with depth, clarity and a sense of total abundance.

By engaging your five senses (sight, hearing, smell, taste and touch), it's possible to take control and stay calm in stressful situations. Consider how a particular smell — such as your grandma's favourite perfume or her famous chicken casserole — can trigger a happy childhood memory. It's incredibly powerful to tap into these types of positive memories on a daily basis, by simply connecting with your senses.

THE 5 SENSES

Sight: Look, acknowledge, see. Notice the view, the formation of clouds, the brilliant colours that are abundant in nature.

Hearing: Listen with closed eyes to what's really happening around you. Also listen to silence; it's powerful and re-energising, and you can hear yourself breathe.

Smell: Your sense of smell can change your hormone levels and promote calmness. Luxurious soap, just-baked bread, freshly ground coffee — all of these scents can alter your state and reduce your stress level.

Taste: Be present during your entire meal and enjoy every bite, such as the taste of a crisp apple, or a hot coffee reaching your belly and how it makes you feel. This is truly the greatest gift to acknowledge in the world of abundance.

Touch: Skin, a soft blanket, a sandy beach, the different textures around us — when you're present and acknowledge them and how they make you feel, you can slow down time.

CREATE YOUR SENSES LIST TO ENRICH YOUR DAILY LIFE

- Tasting a good cup of coffee.
- Splashing your face with warm water.
- Listening to your child giggling.
- Relaxing as hot water from the shower hits your back.
- Smelling a delicious, rich meal in a slow cooker.
- Running your hands through your pet's fur.
- Breathing in the smell of freshly baked cakes or cookies.
- Admiring colourful flowers as they come into bloom.
- Enjoying the scent of the leather interior of a new car.
- Waking to the sounds of birds chirping in the early hours of the day.
- Appreciating the smell of a fresh summer's morning.

"I'm a busy guy, but I set aside quiet time every morning and evening to keep my equilibrium centred on my own path. I don't like being swayed by anything that might be negative or damaging."

- Donald Trump

MY NOTES

_____

_____

_____

_____

_____

_____

_____

_____

_____

_____

_____

_____

_____

_____

_____

_____

_____

"Success is liking yourself, liking what you do, and liking how you do it."

– Maya Angelou

SUCCEED

SUCCEED

By now you've established the foundations of your values, beliefs and behaviours, and you've simplified your visions and goals. Now, you have a clear idea of where you're headed and you know what you want out of life.

You've also developed a solid structure and self-management plan, with lists and time management strategies to keep you on track.

From here, it's all about maintenance. The aim of the game is to enjoy and prepare the next stages of your life so you can face each day with purpose, excitement and quiet confidence, and therefore lead a successful, balanced life.

But before you start striving for success, it's important to identify exactly what success means to you. How do you know if you're successful or on track to achieving success? What does being successful *really* mean — and, just as importantly, how can you measure it in your own life?

There's no right or wrong answer by which you define success. The term itself is subjective; what success means to you is likely to be different from what it means to me, or anyone else. It's crucial that you identify your own personal criteria for success, as achieving success (and feeling successful) is what you want to tap into on a daily basis.

How does it feel?

How would you define your idea of success in one succinct sentence?

Structure your personal success definition into your life:
- Write it in the front of your daily planner.
- Add it to your online calendar.
- Stick it on your fridge.
- Program it into your phone.
- Add it to your vision board.

Success means the freedom of choice in my daily life.

Success is the ability to earn a living from work that I'm passionate about.

Success means living a purposeful life.

Success is when I approve of myself and what I'm doing each day.

MY DEFINITION OF SUCCESS

Success means living the life I choose. When I take responsibility, I feel successful every day. I've structured my diary and chosen how busy I am, how many times I've said yes, how fit I am, what I'm eating, whether my finances are up to date and how I've spent quality time with my family and friends. I've also structured time for stillness, mindfulness and space, and worked my business so my time is used profitably. This gives me a great sense of freedom in my life.

YOUR SUCCESS TOOLKIT

Everyone wants to be successful and significant, and yet so few of us actually reach our goals in such a way that we get to enjoy them.

Your success is your vision, backed with a strategy, followed up by a healthy level of self-confidence and a positive self-image. To keep on track towards living a successful life full of purpose, it's important to create a success toolkit that includes:

1. Acknowledgement
2. Affirmations
3. Confidence maintenance
4. Hobbies
5. Stress management
6. Humour

1. Acknowledgement

It's such a wonderful feeling to recognise who you are and what you achieve. It makes our journey smooth and easy. On a regular basis, whether it's weekly or monthly, write a few lines to keep you in the habit of being positive.

I learnt today...
I'm grateful for...
I'm thankful for...
I can let go of...
I can release the need to be...
I acknowledge myself today for...
I choose to enjoy today because...

- I'm... calm, confident, respected and inspiring.

- I invite... the adventure of the new day ahead, and look forward to the experiences it brings.

- I'll... learn new ways to express myself, new skills to master and new experiences to enjoy.

- I look forward to... this day with abundance and I'll be guided to make great decisions today.

- I'm going to... have a peaceful and calm day with new insights and understanding, and unexpected prosperity coming my way.

"The only place where success comes before work is in the dictionary."

- Vidal Sassoon

2. Affirmations

Success has everything to do with your mindset. Your habits, attitudes and the way you behave every day motivate you and dictate where you expend your energy. If you have a vision at work of flowing profits, industry respect, happy customers and a balanced life, this vision is only achievable if you develop attitudes and habits that support and drive this success.

3. Confidence maintenance

Our mind is in charge of our confidence — if we think positive, strong, caring thoughts and are kind to ourselves, we allow more and new experiences to come in. We have the power to choose our thoughts and they are our future.

- Do activities that boost your confidence — these are energising activities. Eg. Clean out your desk, wash the car or declutter your living room.
- Surround yourself with confident, successful people and learn from them.
- Acknowledge not only the big wins, but also the small daily wins.
- Share your wins with those who support you — not the dream stealers.
- Remember that if you try to control everything, you upset the natural flow. Enjoy the work you've done and let it work for you.

"It's better to hang out with people better than you. Pick out associates whose behaviour is better than yours and you'll drift in that direction."

– Warren Buffet

4. Hobbies

Hobbies need to be developed now — if not sooner! It's vital to foster growth and development in this area. If you develop your hobbies each year, even by only a little bit, then in your spare time you'll be passionate about and skilled at your hobbies.

When people reach their 60s and 70s, many find it hard to start a new hobby. They've worked hard, raised their family and now they have a little more time on their hands — but often it's too late! To start learning how to cook or studying photography at the age of 65 can be daunting, overwhelming and far too hard.

When you look at those who are older than you who are so-called 'retired', the inspiring ones have many passions and interests and bring great knowledge and conversation to the table. They have more than 'work' as an interest.

"I'm worried I'll be bored"

Now aged 65, Elaine was 61 and semi-retired when we first met. A millionaire many times over with a successful real estate business, she and her husband Frank were getting ready to retire. "I'm worried I'll be bored," she told me. "What will I do all day?"

We identified Elaine's interests and passions and set about creating hobbies and regular appointments to provide structure to her life, post-retirement.

- At 6am three mornings a week, Elaine and her husband power walk along the beach.
- On the other mornings, she enjoys working out at the gym or swimming in her pool.
- After a hiatus of over a decade, Elaine began playing tennis again and now meets with a local group each Tuesday.
- On weekends, she enjoys socialising with friends, eating out at restaurants, hosting BBQs or picnics on the couple's boat.
- One day each week, Elaine spends quality time with her two grandsons, which also gives her daughter a chance to work.
- Every four to six months, Elaine and Frank travel overseas. This year it was a cooking tour through Italy; next year it's two weeks at an Ayurvedic clinic in the Maldives.

5. Stress management

Stress is your body's way of responding to any kind of demand. When you feel stressed, your body reacts by releasing chemicals into the blood, which give you more energy and strength. This is a good thing if your stress is caused by clear physical danger, but if it's in response to an emotional stressor, you have no outlet for the extra energy and strength, which is when it can adversely affect both your body and your mind.

People under large amounts of stress can become tired, sick and unable to concentrate or think clearly. Sometimes, they even suffer mental and physical breakdowns.

In times of high stress, one-minute goals are the answer. One minute is a long time!
- Breathe for one minute.
- Stretch for one minute.
- Draw a picture for one minute.
- Drink water for one minute.
- Walk for one minute.
- Close your eyes and count for one minute.
- Gain some perspective for one minute.

Choice

"If you choose resentment you will get more resentment.
If you want joy you need to think joyful thoughts.
If you want prosperity you need to open yourself up mentally.
If you want to flow creatively then you need to open up and believe you are and the universe will allow."

– Louise Hay

"People rarely succeed unless they have fun in what they are doing."

– Dale Carnegie

6. Humour

Humour is what balances out the seriousness of life and it's what helps you to endure challenges. So don't take life too seriously! While it's great to celebrate your achievements and accomplishments, it's just as important to enjoy the journey — and this is where laughter plays a huge role. It may not be a cure-all, but laughter is priceless medicine.

- **Laughter relaxes your whole body.** A good, hearty laugh relieves physical tension and stress, leaving your muscles relaxed for up to 45 minutes afterwards.
- **Laughter triggers the release of endorphins**. The body's natural feel-good chemicals, endorphins promote an overall sense of wellbeing.
- **Laughter boosts the immune system**. It decreases stress hormones and increases immune cells and infection-fighting antibodies, thus improving your resistance to disease.
- **Laughter protects the heart.** Laughter improves the function of blood vessels and increases blood flow, which can help protect against a heart attack and other cardiovascular problems.

MOVING FORWARD

Imagine for a moment that you're standing perfectly still in a typical yoga pose. You have one leg raised, with your foot resting against your knee, and the other foot planted firmly on the ground. Your hands are on your hips for balance. Your eyes are closed, your mind is free and you're focused on nothing else but remaining still and calm.

No matter how good a job you do of holding this position, you'll always be moving, at least a little bit, to maintain your balance.

This is what managing your life is like: just as you need to keep tweaking your posture to keep balanced, you'll need to continue fine-tuning and developing your philosophies, strategies and processes to remain successful.

TRAVEL WITH PURPOSE

When you travel with purpose, more world abundance opens up, more relationships are created — and, most importantly, you look at your bucket list and hobbies, and incorporate them into your trip. Holidays can be amazing experiences when you travel to learn, meet new people and grow as a person, for example when you go on photography tours, art adventures, cooking trips and wine holidays. These are the holidays you talk about the most, because you come home feeling more inspired than ever.

Bucket list

A bucket list is more than a list of goals — it's a compilation of your boldest dreams. You have to work towards your dreams just like you work towards your goals, which is why it's important to write them down. By creating a bucket list, you turn your dreams into attainable, tangible, doable goals to work towards.

To compile your own bucket list, think about the following areas and what you'd like to achieve in each:

CAREER

RECREATION

KNOWLEDGE

ACTIVITIES

TRAVEL

FAMILY

HOME

FRIENDS

ADVENTURE

FITNESS

SPIRITUALITY

INVESTMENTS

EDUCATION

PERSONAL GROWTH

FUN

WRITE A BOOK

SWIM WITH DOLPHINS

PERFORM A STAND-UP COMEDY ROUTINE

JUMP OUT OF A PLANE

COMPLETE A MARATHON

GO CAMPING

CLIMB MOUNT EVEREST

VISIT THE PYRAMIDS OF EGYPT

TAKE YOUR KIDS TO DISNEYLAND

GO BUNGEE JUMPING

PAINT A PAINTING FOR YOUR HOME

SCORE A HOLE IN ONE IN GOLF

GO SCUBA DIVING IN A SHIPWRECK

LEARN TO SALSA DANCE

RIDE A MOTORBIKE ACROSS A COUNTRY

GO ON A SAFARI IN AFRICA

SEE THE SEVEN NATURAL WONDERS OF THE WORLD

ACHIEVE YOUR MBA

LEARN ANOTHER LANGUAGE

READ THE TOP 100 BOOKS OF ALL TIME

WALK ON HOT COALS

VISIT ANTARCTICA

WRITE A SONG

GO ON A HELICOPTER RIDE OVER THE GRAND CANYON

LIVE IN A FOREIGN COUNTRY

BE AN EXTRA IN A MOVIE

VISIT ALL SEVEN CONTINENTS

YOUR 20-YEAR PLAN

Where will you be in 20 years' time? While it's virtually impossible for you to answer this question with any real clarity and depth, it's also quite confronting.

However, if you're 40 years old right now, and someone asks, "Where will you be when you're 60?" a vague picture of what your life may be like begins to emerge. Because an age is attached to the question, by default it gives an age to the people around you — your partner, your children, your parents and your friends. Suddenly, you can see what 'stage' of life you'll be in 20 years into the future, and that helps you to build a picture of what you want your life to look like at that stage.

By creating a 20-year plan as a draft map of your potential future, you begin planting the seeds for what you might accomplish, while at the same time building a structure to support you in reaching for those goals.

CREATE A VISION AND WORK BACKWARDS

- Start with a blank piece of paper or spreadsheet.
- Create four columns: year, career, home and family.
- Input things you're fairly sure of: your age each year, your partner's age, your kids' ages, your stage of life, your health and your career. Once this information is plugged in, it isn't that difficult to open your mind up to dream big.
- List every holiday you dream of taking and every hobby you want to develop. Look at your 20-year plan and work out where your milestone birthdays and anniversaries will fall. Start thinking about the celebrations you'd like to create, and dates when you may be able to match up your dream holiday destinations with major milestones. Would your 15th wedding anniversary be a good time to plan a luxury week in Paris?

Test your comfort zone

1. **Commit:** Get out of your comfort zone as often as possible. If you don't challenge yourself and make yourself a little uncomfortable, you won't grow, evolve and flourish as a human being.

2. **When you're ripe, you rot:** Make sure you're always a little bit 'green', as it means you're still trying new things and have the capacity to learn. And realise that there's always room for improvement.

3. **Crawl, walk, run:** Don't force yourself to leap into the deep end immediately. Break down bigger goals into smaller chunks, and slowly take on more daring challenges.

4. **Be curious:** Throw away your assumptions about what will happen and get curious instead.

5. **Do the opposite:** You know your strengths, so don't play to them. Numbers geek? Try a course in meditation. IT guru? Enrol in cooking classes. Creative thinker? Sign up for martial arts. Open up new sides of yourself and explore them!

"I've failed over and over and over again in my life and that is why I succeed."

– Michael Jordan

HARNESSING YOUR STRATEGY

You've done a lot of work to get to this point. As well as identifying what's really important to you in life, you've built a strong foundation and solid structure that will allow you to accomplish anything you truly desire. In effect, you've developed your life strategy — and now it's time to review and celebrate how far you've come.

Celebration and self-recognition

How do you celebrate reaching your goals, milestones and achievements? In the daily treadmill of life, it's easy to lose sight of the big picture, particularly if an accomplishment comes and goes without you taking the time to acknowledge that you stuck to your plan, you achieved your goals and you're in line with your values, beliefs and visions.

It's imperative for your sense of achievement — and also for continual motivation, energy and thirst to be your optimal best — that you celebrate your progress with exciting rewards. To maintain the energy and drive to continue, every three to six months you need to pause, verbally acknowledge your recent successes and plan to celebrate them.

- Go to your favourite restaurant.
- Enjoy an expensive bottle of wine.
- Spend a full uninterrupted day with your family.
- Share the news with your family, friends and colleagues.
- Give yourself a budget and go shopping.
- Escape your daily grind by taking a day off work.
- Book in at a day spa for the ultimate pamper session.
- Have a weekend away.
- Relax at the beach.
- Spend a day playing golf.

FINISHING TOUCHES

- Setting yourself up to flourish with continual growth.
- Investing in advanced growth.
- Succession plans.
- Dealing with setbacks, self-sabotage and rejections.
- Creating permanent and sustainable change.
- A word on energy — it's physical, mental, emotional and spiritual.

REASSESSING FRIENDSHIPS

Friendships come on many different levels. Every friendship is unique and they're not all equal. Many people fail to realise that the most important friendship you can have is a friendship with yourself, and only then can you welcome other friendships with the people you feel comfortable being yourself.

POWER QUESTIONS

- Is this what I want to be doing?
- What are some of my 'golden moments' in life and how can I repeat them now?
- What's my body trying to tell me?
- Where could I work less and achieve more?
- How am I holding myself back from achieving my true goals?
- What matters to me the most?
- How do I want the world to be different because I lived in it?

"If you realised how powerful your thoughts are, you would never think a negative thought."

- Peace Pilgrim

YOUR RECIPE FOR SUCCESS

- **S: Sort out your values.**
- **U: Understand your beliefs and behaviours.**
- **C: Choose your vision for yourself.**
- **C: Construct goals and strategies to support your vision and brand.**
- **E: Evaluate and acknowledge each step of your journey and progress.**
- **S: Simplify and structure your process.**
- **S: Smile and enjoy your ideal setup for optimal living and success!**

MY NOTES

_____

_____

_____

_____

_____

_____

_____

_____

_____

_____

_____

_____

_____

_____

_____

_____

_____

_____

THE FOUNDATION OF YOU
WHAT DO YOU REALLY WANT?
WHO ARE YOU? **OWN YOUR ACHIEVEMENTS**
RECORD YOUR ACCOMPLISHMENTS
BE MINDFUL **GOLDEN MOMENTS**
YOUR VALUES **THE KEY TO YOU**
FAMILY HAPPINESS WEALTH
ACCOMPLISHMENT ADVENTURE **HEALTH**
GREATEST LESSONS LEARNT
CONQUER LIMITING BELIEFS
CHOOSE YOUR HABITS
SIMPLIFY = CLARITY **BALANCE**
ENERGY DRAINERS GET CLUTTER-FREE
SETTING BOUNDARIES

WINNER'S LIST OPPORTUNITIES

CREATE YOUR VISION CLARIFY YOUR GOALS

STRUCTURE = BALANCE

SELF-MANAGEMENT PRODUCTIVITY

GET INTO THE DRIVER'S SEAT

TAKE RESPONSIBILITY UNDERLYING COMMITMENTS

SELF-SABOTAGE KEY TO FULFILMENT

MOTIVATION **THE 5 SENSES** SIGHT

TOUCH SMELL SOUND TASTE

SUCCESS = FREEDOM

HOW DOES IT FEEL? SUCCESS

TOOLKIT **CALM CONFIDENCE**

CHOICE MANAGING STRESS

"Before you act, listen.
Before you react, think.
Before you spend, earn.
Before you criticise, wait.
Before you pray, forgive.
Before you quit, try."

– Ernest Hemingway

WHAT IS MOST IMPORTANT IN YOUR LIFE?

Most people answer this by saying things such as family, health, friendships and career. Now, imagine each of these as a juggling ball, made of the finest crystal... except the career ball... that one is made of rubber. If this is the case, you should do everything in your power not to drop the most valuable and fragile balls, understanding that work is like a rubber ball that can bounce back if dropped occasionally... and the others can not.

ONE FINAL NOTE...

We all want to be happy. We want to maximise the personal, professional and financial potential that life has to offer, but at the end of the day, we'd prefer to do so without the stress, anxiety and exhaustion that is often bundled up with "success".

We are over-achievers, which means we're usually over-stimulated, with epic "to do" lists, competing priorities and crowded social calendars.

As much as we want to flourish and succeed, sometimes we will fall off that path. That's okay. This book will bring you back to the basics and remind you...

It's as simple as that. Always come back and check in with your foundations.

And that is the purpose of this book. By understanding the strategies outlined in these pages, you can develop your own personal strategy for living your optimal life.

The reality is, it is a learning process, and new lessons will always unfold.

But by developing your personal strategy for success, you take action towards living your best life by declaring that it's not enough to simply "get by", or survive the chaos. That instead, you want to live a remarkable life filled with joy, balance, clarity and calm, leaving you free to truly engage in your daily life and enjoy every success.

The second purpose of this book is to remind you not to be a passenger in life! Jump into the driver's seat and live each day with joy, balance, purpose and clarity, so you can truly engage and enjoy every success.

MY NOTES

MY NOTES

MY NOTES

_____

_____

_____

_____

_____

_____

_____

_____

_____

_____

_____

_____

_____

_____

_____

_____

_____

_____

_____

MY NOTES

MY NOTES

MY NOTES

MY NOTES

MY NOTES

MY NOTES

MY NOTES

As a reader of
Simplify Structure Succeed,
visit the website to sign up for the
gift of a daily motivational thought.

www.shannahkennedy.com

Find out more about Shannah Kennedy and her products and services at:
www.shannahkennedy.com

Order books online and/or book your Simplify Structure Succeed Conference Workshop.
Topics covered:

- Goal setting
- Time management
- Health management
- Personal branding
- Characteristics of success
- Life skills for employees
- Inspiration and motivation
- Creating balance and clarity of purpose
- Future visions and succession planning
- Peak performance and your essential toolbox

Conference workshops are tailored to suit the audience and provide the essential lists.

CONTACT SHANNAH

EMAIL: shannah@shannahkennedy.com
WEB: www.shannahkennedy.com